DATE DUE

The AIDS Awareness Library

Myths and Facts About AIDS

Anna Forbes, MSS

The Rosen Publishing Group's
PowerKids Press
New York

Published in 1996 by The Rosen Publishing Group, Inc.
29 East 21st Street, New York, NY 10010

First Edition

Photo credits: Cover © John Michael/International Stock; p. 4 © Michael Philip Manheim/International Stock; p. 7 © Jeff Greenberg/International Stock; p. 8 © Barbara Kreye/International Stock; p. 11 © George Ancona/International Stock; p. 12 © Robert Burke/Liaison International; p. 15 © Dario Perla/International Stock; p. 16 © Noel Quido/Gamma-Liaison; p. 19 © Carolina Kroon/Impact Visuals; p. 20 © Peter Clemens/International Stock.

Book Design and Layout: Erin McKenna

Forbes, Anna, MSS
     Myths and facts about AIDS / Anna Forbes.—1st ed.
         p.   cm. — (The AIDS awareness library)
     Includes index.
     Summary: Presents simple factual information to dispel misconceptions about HIV and AIDS.
     ISBN 0-8239-2366-5
    1. AIDS (Disease)—Juvenile literature. [1. AIDS (Disease). 2. HIV infections. 3. Diseases.] I. Title.
II. Series.
RC607.A26F63 1996
616.97'92—dc20
                                      96-2500
                                           CIP
                                           AC

Manufactured in the United States of America

Contents

What Are Myths?

This is a book about a disease called AIDS. People are scared of AIDS because it is spreading fast. People who get AIDS die a lot sooner than most people. Some people don't know the facts about AIDS. They believe things that aren't true about the disease. These ideas are called **myths** (MITHS).

The best way to learn the truth about something is to learn the facts. Here are some myths and facts about AIDS.

◀ One way to learn the facts about AIDS is to ask an adult.

Myth: People with AIDS are bad people.

Fact: People with AIDS are like everyone else. Some are good and some are not so good. They got HIV, the **virus** (VY-rus) that causes AIDS, by accident.

Accidents happen when people don't know that they're doing something that isn't safe. They also happen when people know that what they're doing is risky, but do it anyway. But having an accident doesn't mean that a person is bad.

Nobody gets AIDS on purpose. ▶

Myth: Some people deserve to get AIDS.

Fact: Most people with AIDS got HIV from having sex or using drugs. They may not have known how to protect themselves from HIV. Or maybe they chose not to protect themselves just one time.

A small number of people with AIDS, such as babies who got it from their mothers before they were born, could not have protected themselves. But no one with HIV got it on purpose. And nobody "deserves" to get AIDS.

◀ No one deserves to get sick, especially with AIDS.

9

Myth: You can get AIDS from doing everyday things.

Fact: We know more about AIDS than about almost any other illness. We know you can't get it from sharing food with someone who has HIV or AIDS. You can't get it from hugging, touching, or shaking hands. You can't get it from being coughed on or sneezed on by a person who has HIV or AIDS. The most common ways people get HIV or AIDS are by having unsafe sex or by sharing a needle when using drugs.

You can't get AIDS from doing everyday things like kissing someone goodnight. ▶

Myth: Getting a shot can give you AIDS.

Fact: Shots are completely safe when the needle is **sterile** (STARE-il). Sterile means super-clean.

People who use drugs sometimes use needles that aren't sterile. They may use one that has HIV in it from someone else. That's how some people get HIV from needles.

But doctors and nurses use only sterile needles so there is no risk of getting HIV.

◀ You can't get HIV from going to the doctor.

Myth: If one person in a family has AIDS, everyone else will get it.

Fact: HIV is not spread by living together, sharing a bathroom, sharing the same bed, or borrowing each other's clothes.

Do you know someone who has AIDS in their family? Don't avoid that person or their family. Instead, ask if you can help.

You can't get HIV just from living with a person who has HIV or AIDS. ▶

Myth: Bad people made HIV to kill people they didn't like.

Fact: It's scary to think that HIV, the virus that causes AIDS, was made by someone on purpose.

But scientists think HIV was not made on purpose. They think it was something that happened in nature. Sometimes the smallest parts of something, its cells, combine in a strange way. That's called **mutation** (myou-TAY-shun). HIV is most likely the result of a natural mutation.

◀ Doctors and scientists are working hard to find a cure for HIV and AIDS.

Myth: People with HIV die quickly.

Fact: When AIDS was first discovered, we didn't know much about it. We didn't have medicines to help people with AIDS stay well.

Now we know how HIV can cause AIDS. We have medicines to help people fight off AIDS. When people with HIV eat healthy foods and take good care of their bodies, it helps. Many people with HIV live for years and years.

People with HIV try hard to stay healthy by taking medicine and eating healthy foods. ▶

Myth: You can't do anything about it, so why worry about AIDS?

Fact: When you look both ways before crossing the street, you are protecting yourself from being hit by a car. We protect ourselves in a lot of ways. Protecting ourselves keeps us safe from harm. Being safe from harm makes sense. You can protect yourself from getting a harmful disease like AIDS too. The more you know about AIDS, the better you can protect yourself.

◀ You can help protect yourself from
HIV and AIDS by learning the facts.

Myth: Nice people don't talk about AIDS.

Fact: That's like saying nice people don't talk about cancer, drugs, fighting, or other things that hurt people.

Talking helps people to learn more. We need to learn as much as we can about how to prevent hurtful things like AIDS from happening.

There is no cure for AIDS yet. So learning about it is the only way we can stop it from spreading.

Glossary

mutation (myou-TAY-shun) When cells combine in a strange way.

myth (MITH) Story or belief that isn't true.

sterile (STARE-il) Free from germs and viruses.

virus (VY-rus) Bacteria that causes disease.

Index